WOMEN AT WORK

153 Photographs by
LEWIS W. HINE

Edited by Jonathan L. Doherty

George Eastman House, Rochester
in association with
DOVER PUBLICATIONS, INC.
NEW YORK

Frontispiece: "Sorting wads for cartridges. Photo — Hine for U.S. Cartridge Co." (78:743:1; *)

Published in Canada by General Publishing Company, Ltd., 30 Lesmill Road, Don Mills, Toronto, Ontario.
Published in the United Kingdom by Constable and Company, Ltd.

Women at Work: 153 Photographs by Lewis W. Hine, is a new work, first published in 1981 by Dover Publications, Inc., New York, and George Eastman House (International Museum of Photography), Rochester.

Book design by Carol Belanger Grafton

International Standard Book Number: 0-486-24154-8
Library of Congress Catalog Card Number: 80-71098

Manufactured in the United States of America
Dover Publications, Inc.
180 Varick Street
New York, N.Y. 10014

INTRODUCTION

This book contains a selection of photographs of women at work from the Lewis Wickes Hine Collection of the International Museum of Photography at George Eastman House. The photographs comprise a fine historical document on the position of working women from 1907 to 1938.

Lewis Wickes Hine has been widely acclaimed as one of the fathers of social-documentary photography. Originally a teacher, Hine set out to expose many unknown aspects of life in America. Essentially he continued to teach, but he taught a much larger audience. He began by photographing the masses of immigrants arriving at Ellis Island in New York in 1905 and 1906. He moved on to record: life in Pittsburgh (for *The Pittsburgh Survey*); the slums of Washington, New York and Chicago; piecework done at home in the New York tenements; child labor (for the National Child Labor Committee); Army and Navy training camps; the effects of World War I in France and the Balkans; southern Blacks; the American worker; rural health services in New York State; the Shelton Looms; the construction of the Empire State Building; flood and drought relief (for the American Red Cross); the Tennessee Valley Authority projects; and reemployment possibilities and technological change (for the National Research Project of the Works Progress Administration). Between these larger projects were interspersed some smaller ones. Hine's lifework clearly presents a wide section of thirty-five years of American history for all to see. Of all these photographs, the pictures of Ellis Island in 1905–6 and again in 1926, of children laboring in the mills, canneries and sweatshops of the East, and of the construction of the Empire State Building are among the best known. These were only three, however, of the many fine photographic projects which Hine undertook during his long and prolific career.

Most of the critical attention paid to Hine's work has been focused on what are considered his "reform" photographs, those which show the evils of the industrial society — slums, tenements and tiny children behind giant looms. Much of Hine's time, however, was spent photographing and affirming positive aspects of society, such as the character of the American worker. Hine's interest in the worker is shown throughout his pictures and writings. One of Hine's first photographs, that of an old-time printer dated 1905, is entitled "The Joy of Work."[1]

Shortly before Hine died in 1940, he proposed a project of photographing American craftsmen. Between those dates he was quite often involved in documenting some aspect of labor; witness his work for the National Child Labor Committee; his photographing of steel workers in Pittsburgh, sweatshop workers in New York City and workers in a variety of industries during the 1920s; as well as his connection with the Empire State Building, Shelton Looms, the TVA and the WPA. In fact, by 1920 Hine had begun to dedicate himself almost exclusively to documentation of the worker in America. Although he wavered occasionally after this time, usually when in need of money, showing the human side of industry became his main concern.

Hine did not photograph women exclusively. Rather he photographed men as well as women in all the industries, sweatshops, homes and trades in which he found them. The photographs in the present volume are a fraction of Lewis Hine's documentation of the American worker, although they do span the whole range of his career. Thus the reform as well as affirming photographs are included in this study.

While looking at Hine's photographs of working women it would be useful to have some idea of the photographer's personal views on the subject. Because Hine was not primarily a writer and only infrequently spelled out his opinions in essay form, his views have to be inferred from other materials: the uses of his photographs in publications; his comments written on the backs of the prints; his philosophy on the worker in general; and of course the prints themselves.

The greatest showing of Lewis Hine's photographs undoubtedly occurred in the pages of Paul Kellogg's magazine *The Survey*. Hine photographs first appeared in *The Survey* (then *Charities and the Commons*) in 1907.[2] Between then and 1940 Hine's work appeared on at least 189 separate occasions in *Charities and the Commons, The Survey* or *Survey Graphic* and was the cover illustration for 34 issues.[3]

Under Paul Kellogg's editorship *The Survey* was in many ways the official organ through which the social-welfare community voiced its opinions. The early 1900s were characterized by the creation of organizations such as the Women's Trade Union League (1903) and the National Child Labor Committee (1904). During the progressive era, a time of great social reform, Paul Kellogg managed to include articles and reports written by many of the great voices in the social-welfare and reform movements. The use of Hine's photographs was perhaps greatest during this time. Most relevant to our own subject, his work illustrated many articles and books on women's working conditions.

In 1907–8 an extensive examination of life in the steel districts of Pittsburgh was made under the direction of Paul Kellogg for the Russell Sage Foundation. Hine was engaged by Kellogg to photograph the workers, home life and industry of the city. The results were published in a six-volume edition entitled *The Pittsburgh Survey*.[4] Two of the volumes deal with women, one exclusively. The examination of women's working conditions was published both in Elizabeth Beardsley Butler's volume of the survey, *Women and the Trades* (1909), and as a series of articles in *Charities and the Commons*. Hine's photographs illustrated them all. *The Pittsburgh Survey* was the first great sociological study of an entire city undertaken in the United States, and the contents are of historical significance today. In her article "The Industrial Environment of Pittsburgh's Women," Butler reported and analyzed pay scales and the life that they could provide for working women. Of one worker she wrote: "A bolt trimmer is paid by the piece for feeding a rounded bolt into the press that squares its end. If she misses no motion of the machine, she repeats this single operation 16,000 times in ten hours and her pay is 96 cents a day." A wage of seven dollars a week was calculated by Butler to provide subsistence with nothing left for washing, sundries, medicine or recreation—in other words, a "barren life."[5]

The Survey also published examinations of tenement-house homework and the irregular employment of women in New York City.[6] These were in the same investigatory style as *The Pittsburgh Survey*, as were also four books authored by Mary Van Kleeck on artificial-flower makers, and women in the bookbinding trade, the millinery trade and evening schools.[7] All of these included photographs of women at work by Lewis Hine.

The inclusion of Hine's prints in works such as those mentioned above does not, of course, prove that Hine shared the same social, political and economic concerns that the women authors held. It is important to realize, however, that at this time Hine was surrounded by, and working intimately with, some of the leaders of the reform movement, most notably: John Spargo, socialist author of *The Bitter Cry of the Children*; Owen Lovejoy, Chairman of the NCLC; Homer Folks of the American Red Cross; Florence Kelly of the National Consumer's League; Paul and Arthur Kellogg of *The Survey*; and the many authors of *The Pittsburgh Survey*. Furthermore, during his tenure with the NCLC Hine himself violently criticized, with both pictures and words, those who allowed or encouraged child labor to continue. He understood and wrote about the economic aspects and implications of child labor.[8] His photographic statements against sweatshops and tenement houses are equally critical. This is not to imply that Hine agreed with all the intellectual beliefs of the reform leaders (although he may have), but rather it suggests that the goals behind his photography were at that time much the same as those of leading reformers of the period.

About 1920 Hine turned his attention to making "work portraits"—photographic interpretations of the worker in industry. These photographs were also published in *The Survey* and *Survey Graphic*, but in a slightly different form. The work portraits were reproduced over several pages in groups pertaining to a single industry, with little accompanying texts. Essentially, they constituted picture essays.[9] With some exceptions, the investigatory role of Hine's pictures declined. The photographs were now more positive in regard to the value of the work pictured. With the lack of text accompanying the pictures in the publications, less knowledge of Hine's opinions of women workers can be gained from this medium. One exception is found in a group of photographs titled "Postal Service in the Big City." A paragraph, almost surely written by Hine, describes two women working in a large post office:

> With their quick eyes and deft hands, women are every day becoming more valuable in the exacting work of the postal service, although as yet they are greatly in the minority as far as numbers are concerned. As in many other activities, war necessity proved how excellently dependable they are.[10]

Although Hine has not here stated a radical viewpoint, this quotation shows that the photographer is accepting women workers and affirming their right to work. The photographs themselves make it evident that this interpretation of his viewpoint is true. With Hine's acknowledged ability to criticize by means of photographs, we would know it if he believed that women did not belong in industry.

In his early years with the NCLC, Hine took notes about the name, height, age and employer of each of his young subjects. This information was later recorded in the form of extensive captions on the back of the prints. Hine continued to write data and captions on prints throughout his life. Unfortunately, many of the photographs of working women do not have as much information with them as one would like. A fair number of them do have "Women—work" written on the back. In the same period, Hine was labeling photographs of male workers "Men at Work." Generally speaking, these terms were not intended as titles of individual prints or collections of prints, but rather constituted a classification system used by the photographer to organize his photographs. Accordingly some pictures are labeled "also in textiles" or "also in paper," referring to the industry of the worker.[11] In 1932 Hine published a book entitled *Men at Work*[12] as a glorification of the male worker in industry. The book was well received by reviewers of the time. Although there is no indication in Hine's correspondence that he intended or wanted to publish a *Women at Work*,[13] the possibility may have existed.

Some idea of Hine's views on the status of women can, however, be gained from the specific captions or titles of a few prints, and one in particular. Hine labeled the photograph of a housewife in the kitchen: "The home-maker deserves recognition as one of our workers." This is a belief that certainly was not generally accepted during the early 1920s when Hine voiced it and, of course, is not completely accepted today. Hine's viewpoint can be considered fairly progressive. In fact, the first group to recognize the significance of women's unpaid labor in the home was the Socialist Party in the early 1900s.[14]

A full understanding of Lewis Hine's social philosophy on women at work, and workers in general, comes from the photographs themselves. Humanity is evident throughout. Look at Hine's pictures of the women doing homework in filthy tenement dwellings, the unsmiling faces of the early sweatshop garment workers and the smiling faces of the women photographed ten to fifteen years later, the beauty of the weaver's hands among the threads of her loom in the photograph at Shelton Looms, and the respect for the woman of 72 y[ea]rs—40 at machine."[15] In the photographs of working women, from the dirty sweatshops to the sparkling Shelton Looms, as in all of Hine's work, the photographer's concern and respect for people, their desperate plights and their fine qualities, remains clear. It is the constant characteristic of Lewis Hine's entire photographic œuvre.

This selection of photographs of women at work contains the same elements that one would find in an examination of all Hine's prints of labor and industry. Although Hine's photographs are tied together by the common thread of concern and respect, there are in a sense two kinds of photographs, both in this book and in Hine's lifework as a whole. Most, but not all, of Hine's work photographs taken before World War I show working conditions that are less than ideal. The lack of sanitation is clearly depicted in Hine's early photographs, where tenement children pick nutmeats for future sale with their teeth and women work in the steaming sweatshops. His criticism of this treatment of humanity is apparent both from the prints and from his written comments on the back of them. Hine's photographs were instrumental in bringing about public recognition of the many evils of the working world. These reforming prints have received just recognition when they were new and ever since. Hine himself viewed this aspect of his work as "negative documentation," showing the "things that had to be corrected."[16]

The second sort of Hine labor photograph reflects the photographer's strong belief in the value of the worker. For the strongest statement of this view we must look to Hine's only book, *Men at Work*. Hine quoted from William James's "The Moral Equivalent of War" for an introductory paragraph:

> Not in clanging fights and desperate marches only is heroism to be looked for, but on every bridge and building that is going up today, on freight trains, on vessels and lumber-rafts, in mines, among fishermen and policemen, the demand for courage is incessant and the supply never fails. These are our soldiers, our sustainers, the very parents of our life.[17]

In a letter to Paul Kellogg Hine acknowledged this as his credo.[18] Hine visualized the American worker as a heroic figure, one who should take great pride in his or her work. The worker was not and could not be dwarfed by the product or the process. In Hine's labor photographs of the 1920s and early 1930s we can see this clearly. The criticism of working conditions found in his earlier photographs is replaced by studies of the worker's power, grace, skill and control. Among the photographs of women workers this is best seen in the Shelton Looms series. It is unfortunate that the glorification of the woman worker is not as powerful as that of the male worker. Presumably this is because women during this time were not employed in the more majestic, romantic or heroic occupations in which many men were found—the steel and construction industries, for example.

Hine saw the photographs of this type as "positive documentation" and believed them to be as important as his earlier work. His social concerns were most certainly still present. In 1938 Hine remembered: "I wanted to do something positive. So I said to myself, 'Why not do the worker at work? The man on the job.' At that time, he was as underprivileged as the kid in the mill."[19] It is important and interesting to note here that rarely, if ever, do any of Hine's photographs deal with the assembly line. The assembly line, satirized so well by Charles Chaplin's 1936 film *Modern Times*, was, and is, surely the place of the worker's greatest alienation from the work process. To show this, however, might have gone against Hine's preference at that time for positive documentation. Hine's goals for his pictures were certainly big ones. Using photographs of the worker in the work place, Hine was ready to show workers and employers the value of the human in the production process. In effect he wanted to help solve labor relations problems between workers and employers:

> "As I see it, the great problem of industry is to go a step beyond merely having the employer and employee get along. The employee must be induced to feel a pride in his work. . . . I try to do with the camera what the writer does with words. People can be stirred to a realization of the values of life by writing. Unfortunately many persons don't comprehend good writing. On the other hand, a picture makes its appeal to everyone. Put into the picture an idea and, if properly used, it may be transferred to the brain of the worker. . . . Interpretive photography . . . will do that, I know, for it has been done. The great problem, of course, is to link the employer and employees in this method of education so that each sees the value in it. The employer must think of it as genuine, not paternalistic; the employee must think of it as a sincere treatment of him and his work, no flattery."[20]

Although it is unlikely that Hine could have solved the major problems of labor and industry, he must be credited with an incredibly bold plan. Again Hine produced a first. The use of photographs for the purposes outlined above is truly propagandistic — not in the negative sense of the word, but rather in its true meaning: the use of a medium or idea to influence a people in a certain direction of thoughts and actions. Hine had done this in his work with the NCLC by showing what was evil. Now he tried to do it for the worker by showing what was good and valuable.

Every author who has written on Hine's work has recognized the photographer's commitment to the human subjects in his pictures. It is unfortunate, however, that most writers of late have concentrated on Hine's negative documentation while devaluing his positive work. During the 1920s and early 1930s Hine's work portraits were well received. Although he was unable to get industry to support his photography, except in the case of the Shelton Looms, he was praised by the editors of *The Survey* as the greatest industrial photographer of all time and furthermore received several important advertising awards for his work.[21] Beaumont Newhall, in 1938, was perhaps one of the last to acknowledge the importance of Hine's later photographs: "Positive documentation is less obvious, more difficult, just as necessary for sociological purposes, and offers much greater range and scope. In this form of documentation also, Hine is a pioneer."[22]

Perhaps the most important things to remember about Lewis Hine and his photography are that Hine was one of the first to use his photographs to promote sociological change, whether by criticizing or affirming, and certainly the first to enjoy such wide publication and use of his prints. Hine's progressive views and human conscience influenced and essentially caused his photography. The result is an immense document of the human side of American life from 1905 to 1940.

NOTES

1. See Lewis W. Hine Collection at the International Museum of Photography at George Eastman House (IMPGEH), Rochester, New York.

2. "The Newsboy at Night in Philadelphia," *Charities and the Commons* 17 (Mar. 9) 1044–6, 1907.

3. Brooklyn Museum, *America and Lewis Hine*; foreword by Walter Rosenblum, biographical notes by Naomi Rosenblum, essay by Alan Trachtenberg; New York: Aperture, 1977, 142 pp.

4. *The Pittsburgh Survey*; ed. Paul Kellogg; New York: Charities Publications Committee, 1909 ff.

5. Elizabeth Beardsley Butler, "Pittsburgh's Steam Laundry Workers," *Charities and the Commons* 20 (Aug. 1) 549–63, 1908.

6. Louise C. Odencrantz, "The Irregularity of Employment of Women Factory Workers," *The Survey* 22 (May 1) 196–210, 1909; Elizabeth C. Watson, "Homework in the Tenements," *The Survey* 25 (Feb. 4) 772–9, 1911.

7. Mary Van Kleeck, *Artificial Flower Makers* (1913); *Women in the Bookbinding Trade* (1913); *Working Girls in Evening Schools* (1914); *A Seasonal Industry: A Study of the Millinery Trade in New York* (1917). All were published in New York by Survey Associates (Russell Sage Foundation).

8. Lewis Wickes Hine, "Child Labor in the Gulf Coast Canneries," *American Academy of Social Science Annals* (July) 118–22, 1911.

9. See: "The Railroaders: Work Portraits," *Survey Graphic* 47 (Oct. 29) 159–66, 1921; "The Powermakers: Work Portraits," *Survey Graphic* 47 (Dec. 31) 511–8, 1921.

10. "Postal Service in the Big City," *Survey Graphic* 48 (July 1) 456, 1922.

11. See Lewis Wickes Hine Collection at IMPGEH, Rochester, New York.

12. Lewis Wickes Hine, *Men at Work*; New York: Macmillan, 1932; reprinted by Dover Publications, New York, 1977.

13. See Lewis Wickes Hine correspondence, IMPGEH, Rochester, New York; and Survey Associates Papers, Social Welfare History Archives, University of Minnesota Libraries, Minneapolis, Minnesota.

14. Rosalyn Baxandall, Linda Gordon and Susan Reverby, *America's Working Women: A Documentary History—1600 to the Present*; New York: Vintage Books, 1976, 210.

15. Photograph reproduced on page 83.

16. Elizabeth McCausland, "Portrait of a Photographer," *Survey Graphic* (Oct.) 503, 1938.

17. Lewis Wickes Hine, *Men at Work*, 1.

18. Letter from Lewis Wickes Hine to Paul Underwood Kellogg, September 8, 1932; Social Welfare History Archives, University of Minnesota Libraries, Minneapolis, Minnesota.

19. Elizabeth McCausland, *op. cit.*

20. "He Photo-interprets Big Labor," *The Mentor* 14 (Sept.) 41–7, 1926.

21. Brooklyn Museum, *op. cit.*

22. Beaumont Newhall, "Lewis Hine," *Magazine of Art* 31 (Nov.) 637, 1938.

CONTENTS

The Frontispiece belongs to the Miscellaneous group of Section II.

NOTE ON THE CAPTIONS

Words in quotation marks represent Hine's own handwritten or typed titles located on the backs of the respective photoprints (whether the precise print used for reproduction in the present volume or some other existing print of the same image; in a very few cases, the captions are drawn from the publications in which the photos were originally reproduced). Captions without quotation marks are supplied by the editor. Dates are given only when available; those within the quotation marks are Hine's. Three kinds of information will be found within parentheses: the International Museum of Photography (George Eastman House) accession numbers of the prints (given for all items); the IMP negative numbers (wherever available); and (where applicable) an asterisk indicating that Hine wrote the words "Women—work" on the backs of those particular prints (this may very well have been merely a filing classification, but it is also possible that he intended a companion publication to his famous *Men at Work* of 1932).

1907-1917
(Illus. 1-47)

Shortly after Hine finished his work at Ellis Island in 1905-6, he was hired by the National Child Labor Committee (NCLC) to document take-home piecework in the New York City tenement houses (see Illus. 1-6). In the streets he found women and children carrying work to their homes. In the tenements his photographs show families, except the fathers, working late into the evening and night making artificial flowers, picking nutmeats and at a variety of other tasks. In her investigation of homework in the tenements, Mary Van Kleeck interviewed a woman able to work on artificial flowers with exceptional speed:

> Sometimes I can make $1.50 and sometimes $3.00 a day. You can't count home work by the day, for a day is really two days sometimes, because people work half the night. When the boss asks me how many flowers I can make in a day I say I cannot tell, but I know how many I can do in an hour. Some girls are so foolish. I've heard them praising themselves and telling the boss that they did the work in a day. They're ashamed to say they worked in the night too. But they only hurt themselves, for the boss says if they earn that much in a day he can cut the price.[1]

It is noteworthy that the man of the family is rarely found participating in homework. Presumably, the man has already put in his hard day's work. Although some of these photographs were intended as indictments of child labor, they are relevant here because of the position of the wife and mother that they depict.

Late in 1907 Hine was engaged by Paul Kellogg, editor of *The Pittsburgh Survey*, to photograph all aspects of life in and around the city of Pittsburgh (Illus. 7-11). Hine's work was combined with six volumes of written material to produce this ex-tremely significant sociological study. At least two volumes are relevant to our topic: Margaret F. Byington's *Homestead: The Households of a Mill Town* and Elizabeth Beardsley Butler's *Women and the Trades*. Some of Hine's photographs used in the latter volume are reproduced in the present book.

The terrible conditions of the sweatshops of New York City were also the targets of Hine's camera during this period (Illus. 12-21). Many of the women and men of the sweatshops worked in the large garment industry. Others were found making cigars or artificial flowers. The features that all sweatshops held in common were "insanitary condi-tions, excessively long hours, and extremely low wages."[2] Most of the workers were immigrants who had traveled through the gates of Ellis Island since the 1890s. In many cases the workers were predom-inantly women. Although this was a time of great outcry from middle-class women for the right to work outside the home, the conditions of the sweat-shops were so poor that the women working there yearned only for marriage and the chance to get out of work.[3] The workers and true conditions of the in-famous sweatshops are documented in Lewis Hine's photographs.

Between 1909 and 1917 Hine traveled through-out the eastern United States photographing and in-vestigating for the NCLC. During this time he also made many photographs of adult industrial workers (Illus. 22-47). In the textile mills of New England and the Carolinas, Hine found whole families work-ing long hours just to make enough money to sur-vive. He photographed garment workers, the paper-box manufacturers with their dangerous cut-ting machines, street vendors, workers in binderies and print shops, and a variety of other trades.

[1]From Rosalyn Baxandall, Linda Gordon and Susan Reverby, *America's Working Women: A Documentary History—1600 to the Present*; New York: Vintage Books, 1976, 163.

[2]*Ibid.*, 101.

[3]Daniel T. Rodgers, *The Work Ethic in Industrial America 1850–1920*; Chicago: University of Chicago Press, 1978, 207.

2

1. "Newly arrived — Textile worker out of a job." (78:1049:
14) 2. "Italian immigrant, East Side, New York City. 1910."
(78:1051:7) OVERLEAF: 3. "Family making artificial flower
wreaths in their tenement house. The little 3 year old on the
left was actually helping, putting the center of the flower into
the petal, and the family said she often works irregularly until 8 P.M. The other children 9, 11 and 14 work until 10 P.M."
Ca. 1908. (78:180:24; IMP NEG 24509)

3

4

5

6

4. "Picking nut meats with dirty baby in lap. Neighbors helping. One girl is cracking nuts with her teeth, not an uncom-
mon sight. New York City. 1911." (78:1051:4; IMP NEG 6457)
5. "N.Y. — 19   ." (78:1027:24; IMP NEG 3205; *) 6. Women
carrying take-home piecework. (78:1051:6)

7

7. "Making old-fashioned 'stogies' Pittsburgh" [caption on this print]. "Working at the suction table" [caption in *Women and the Trades*]. (77:187:99; *) **8.** "Etching glass. Pgh" [caption on this print]. "Glass decorators. By polishing the glass on a revolving wheel the decorator brings out the brilliancy of the ruby color" [caption in *Women and the Trades*]. (77: 187:105; *)

9

10

10

11

9. "Packing olives in a cannery, old style" [caption on this print]. "Bottling olives with a grooved stick" [caption in *Women and the Trades*]. (77:187:97; *) 10. Young girl working in a bottle factory. (77:184:5mp; *) 11. "Filling and capping mustard jars" [caption in *Women and the Trades*]. (77:187:96; *)

12. "Artificial flower factory." (78:1052:42;
IMP NEG 19021)

13

14

15

13. "Woman making cigars, Tampa, Florida." Ca. 1910–12. (78:1014:62; IMP NEG 10275) 14. "Italian making artificial flowers." (78:1052:27) 15. "A corner in an old-time sweatshop. 1910." (78:1052:14; IMP NEG 3788; *)

16

16. "Old-time sweatshop, N.Y. 1910 or 1912." (78:1052:16; IMP NEG 3793) **17.** Sewing garments in a sweatshop. (78: 1052:19; IMP NEG 5140)

18

19

18. "Young laundry worker. 1913." (78:1052:39; *) 19. "Coat-maker in N.Y. sweatshop. 1909." (78:1052:18; IMP NEG 4351) 20. "Small garment shop in N.Y. Tenement. c. 1908." (78:1052:2) 21. Women working in a laundry. (78:1014: 237)

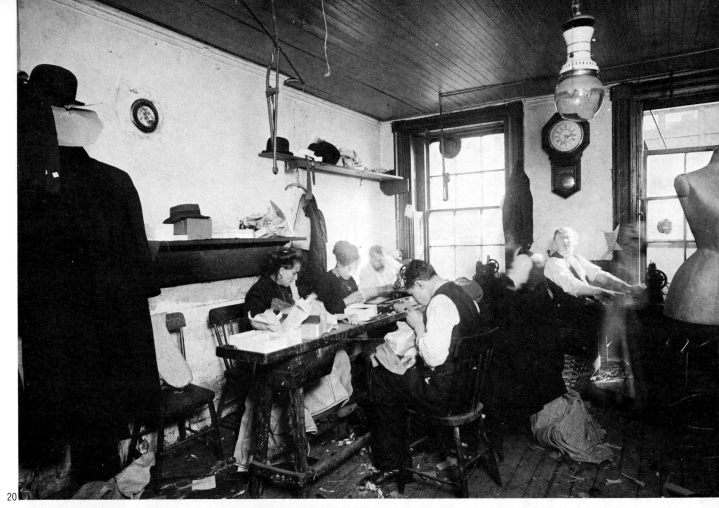

20

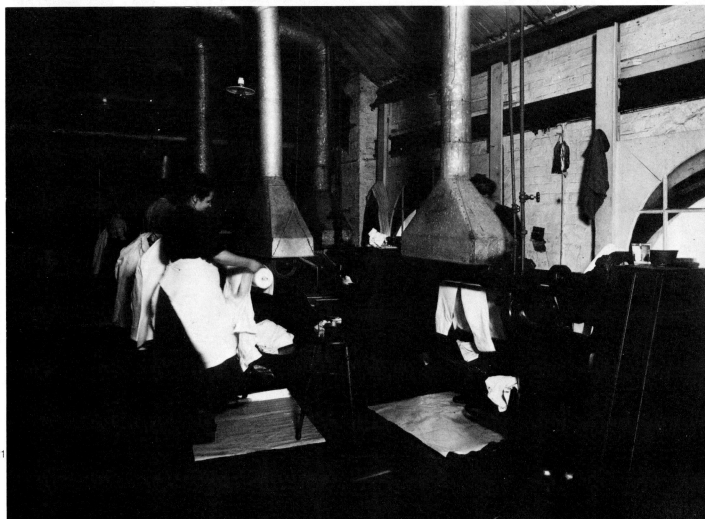

21

23

22. "In an old-fashioned textile mill. Spinner. 1912" [caption in this print]. "Old spinner in a Georgia mill" [on another print]. (78:1005:21;*) 23. Young girl working on stockings in knitting mill. (78:990:48)

22

21

24

25

26

24. "Textile worker New England." (78:1005:11) 25. "Cotton Mill — Spooling — South 1910." (78:1005:13) 26. "At Loom." (72:159:224mp)

27

28

29

27. "Jewish clothing worker. The Song of the Shirt. Rochester, N.Y. 1915." (78:990:13; IMP NEG 6777) **28.** "Italian Garment maker." (78:990:2; IMP NEG 27123) **29.** "Clothing factory, N.Y." (78:990:6; IMP NEG 5141; *)

30

31

30. Women workers in a paper-box
factory. (78:1014:55; IMP NEG 20920;*)
31. "Paper box maker." (78:1014:61;*)
32. "Making paper boxes." (78:1014:
59) 33. Worker in a paper-box factory.
(78:1014:58; IMP NEG 20148;*)

32

33

35

34. "Making paper-boxes." (78:1014:44; *)
35. Young worker in a paper-box factory. (78:1014:57; *) 36. Making paper boxes. (3122mp)

38

37. "A corner in a modern printing shop." (78:996:21)
38. Young print-shop worker. (78:996:23; *)

39

40

39. Worker in a print shop. (78:996:22) 40. "Binding books in the modern machine way." (78:996:24; *) 41. Stitching straw hats. (3119mp) OVERLEAF: 42. Wrapping packages in a department store. (3117mp)

43

44

45

43. Women selling vegetables at an outdoor market. (78:
1028:33) 44. "German truck gardener." (78:1000:1; *) 45.
Decorating glass tumblers. (78:1014:238)

46

46. "Candy worker, New York." (78:1014:242) **47.** "Rags" [paper
industry?]. (78:1014:168)   47

1920-1938
(Illus. 48-152 and Frontispiece)

After World War I, Hine moved to almost exclusive documentation of labor and industry. There are occasional exceptions, probably due to the hard financial times that Hine encountered for the last twenty years of his life. The three photographs of black women in a print shop are part of a little-known series Hine made somewhere in the South around 1920 (Illus. 48–53). Most of this series does not deal with the worker. The photographs of garment makers of the Amalgamated Clothing Workers Union (Illus. 92–110) are not dated but were undoubtedly made during the 1930s. Aside from his documentation of various industries as a whole, Hine occasionally made photographs for particular firms. Of these images, those shown here include photographs for the U.S. Cartridge Corporation (Frontispiece), the Miniature Incandescent Lamp Company (Illus. 60–64) and Western Electric (Illus. 65–72 & 85).

Lewis Hine's relationship with Sidney Blumenthal, president of the Shelton Looms of Shelton, Connecticut, was certainly the most valuable and productive association with private industry that he developed (Illus. 111–118). Blumenthal was considered by Hine, and probably was, one of the more progressive leaders in the management of industry. In a 1917 article he had advocated company-provided disability compensation, life insurance and pensions.[1] In 1933 Hine photographed all aspects of the manufacture of fine fabrics at the Shelton Looms. Out of this work came a portfolio of photographs and some text entitled: *Through the Threads of the Shelton Looms*.[2] Both Blumenthal and Hine received many requests for additional prints after the original edition appeared. Unfortunately, copies of the entire portfolio are very difficult to locate today. The prints reproduced here and labeled "Shelton Looms" are, however, photographs from the series, some of which were undoubtedly in the portfolio. Fittingly, Blumenthal characterized Hine as an "artist, photographer, and idealist of the human in industry."[3]

In the fall of 1933 Hine was hired by Arthur E. Morgan of the Tennessee Valley Authority (TVA) to document the progress of the great Tennessee electrical project (Illus. 119–125). Hine put in a preliminary month with the TVA in October and November 1933. The photographs produced during that time show the construction of the dams, the workers, rural homesteads, and many of the people in the area to be affected by the TVA project. After Hine returned from Tennessee, disputes developed between the photographer and Morgan over further documentary goals and the crediting of pictures. The latter problem turned out to be too great, and Hine broke off his relationship with the agency.[4] The Hine TVA photographs reproduced in the present volume are a selection of those showing working women. The depiction of women was not likely a specific goal of the TVA in their hiring of Hine.

The last photographs in this collection (Illus. 126–152) are from Hine's work in 1936–7 as Chief Photographer of the Works Progress Administration's National Research Project on Reemployment Opportunities and Recent Changes in Industrial Techniques.[5] With David Weintraub, Director of the project, Hine traveled through Massachusetts, New Jersey and Pennsylvania documenting the effects of growing technology on the workers of many industries. In many cases Hine's photographs showed the difference between the way a product had been made in the past through skill and craftsmanship and the way it was created in 1936–7 on an automated production line. It is interesting to note that these photographs are somewhat of a return to investigatory photography in that they were intended, and used, to show how growing technology had cost some workers their jobs and others their craftsmanship.[6]

[1]Sidney Blumenthal, "Human Engineering Department in a Textile Mill," *Textile World Journal* (Jan.) 13, 1917.

[2]*Through the Threads of the Shelton Looms*; New York: Sidney Blumenthal and Co., Inc., 1933.

[3]Letter from Sidney Blumenthal to Arthur E. Morgan, August 21, 1933; Social Welfare History Archives, University of Minnesota Libraries, Minneapolis, Minnesota.

[4]Letter from Lewis Wickes Hine to Paul Underwood Kellogg, October 29, 1934; Social Welfare History Archives, University of Minnesota Libraries, Minneapolis, Minnesota.

[5]See: David Weintraub and Lewis Hine, *Technological Change*; Philadelphia: National Research Project of Works Progress Administration, 1937; "Manpower Skills," *Survey Graphic* **26** (May) 275–9, 1937.

[6]*Ibid.*

49

50

48. "This negro girl was an expert linotyper in a southern publishing house. 1920." (78:1034:98; IMP NEG 16682) 49. Tobacco worker. (78:1034:1; IMP NEG 12823) 50. Tobacco (?) workers. (78:1034:3)

51

52

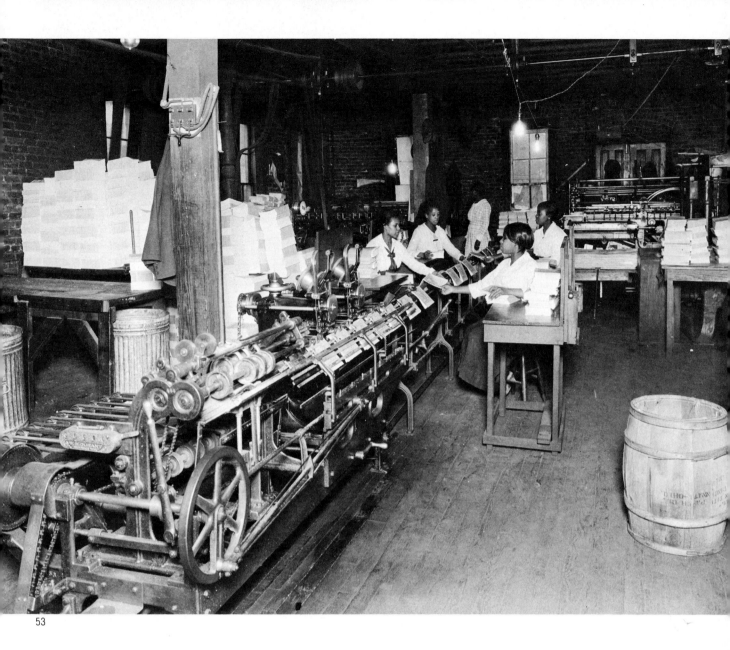

53

51. "A frugal negro home in southern community. 1920." (78:1034:103; IMP NEG 11937) 52. Black woman setting type in a southern print shop. (78:1034:93; IMP NEG 21077) 53. "Negro workers in a well-managed print-shop in a southern community. 1920." (78:1034:97)

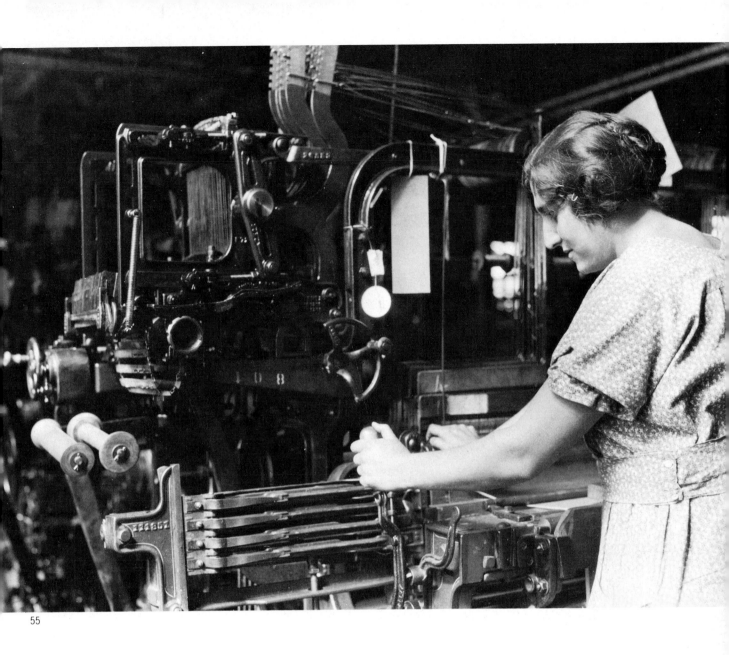

55

54. Textile worker. (78:1005:34) 55. "Modern power loom
in New Jersey silk mill. 1920." (78:1005:32; *)

56

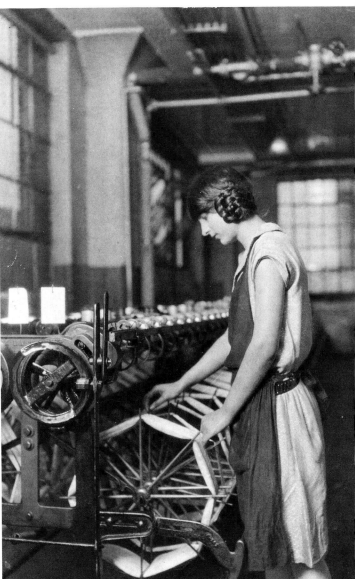

57

56. Worker in a textile mill. (78:1005:40) 57. Worker in a textile mill. (78:1005:35) 58. Weaver in a textile mill. (78: 1005:52; IMP NEG 19046; *) 59. Worker in a textile mill. (78: 1005:71)

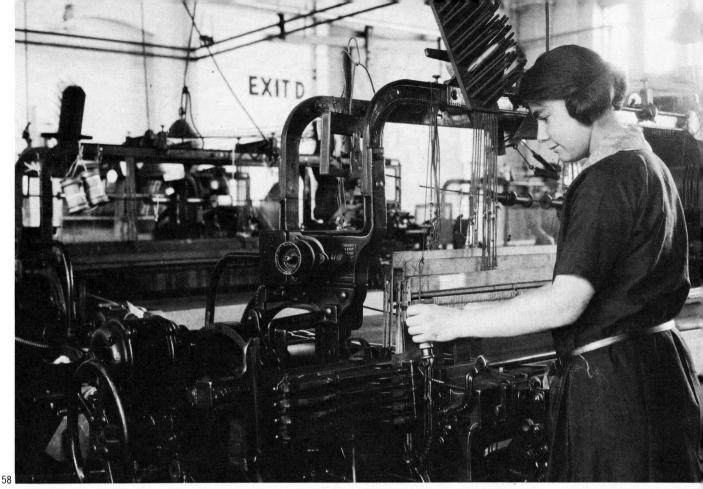

58

59

60. Worker at Miniature Incandescent Lamp Corporation. (78:745:6)

61

62

61. "Adjusting filament in electric bulbs." (78:745:7) **62.** Inserting filaments in small light bulbs. For Miniature Incandescent Lamp Corporation. (78:745:1)

63

63. "Blowing bulbs for auto lamps." For Miniature Incandescent Lamp Corporation. (78:745:2) 64. "Making small autobulbs." For Miniature Incandescent Lamp Corporation. (78:745:10; *)

65. "Testing telephone cables." (78:750:26; *) **66.** "Women worker making parts for telephones." (78:750:32; *)

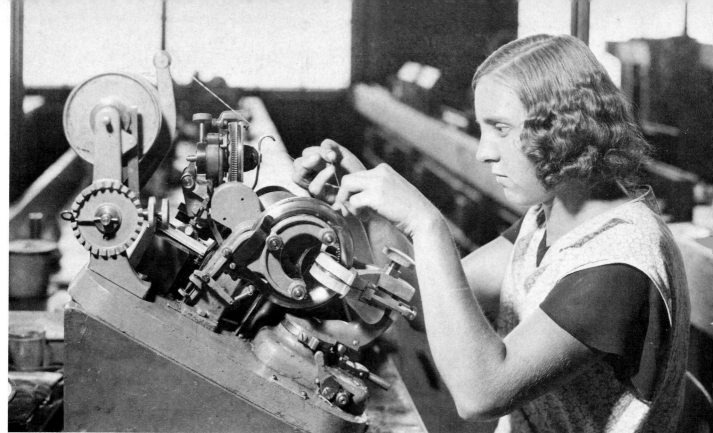

67

68

67. Worker in a telephone factory. (78:750:30; *) 68.
"A Madonna of the Machine." For Western Electric.
(78:749:2; *) OVERLEAF: 69. "Central phone exchange."
(78:750:3)

70. "Operator and supervisor in a N.Y. 'Central.'" (78:750:7) 71. Light punch press operator. For Western Electric. (78:749:15) 72. Operator in a New York "Central." (78:750:2)

74

75

73. "Scrublady, N.Y. 1920." (78:1014:146) 74. Woman working in a laboratory. (78:1014:79) 75. Assembling batteries in a factory. (78:1014:46; *)

76

77

78

76. Woman working in a laboratory. (78:1014:80) 77."Telegraph Operator. Americans at Work." (78:1014:153) 78. Factory worker (making garlands?). (78:1014:67)

80

81

79. "The home-maker deserves recognition as one of our workers." (78:1053:6) 80. Cook in a large kitchen. (78:1014:120) 81. Young girl apprentice polishing metal platter. (72:159:1196mp)

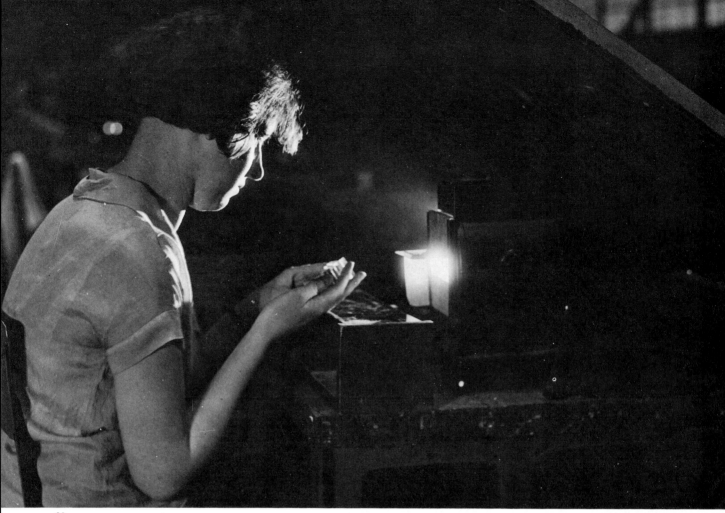

82

83

82. Inspecting lens blanks. (78:1014:50) 83. Woman at typewriter. (78:1014:149) 84. "Designer for Jewelry, N.Y." (78:1014:228; *)

85

86

87

85. Factory work for Western Electric. (78:749:22) 86. Tire manufacturing. (78:1014:45) 87. "Sorting and brushing the skins for felt hats (N.Y.)." (78:1003:31; *) OVERLEAF: 88. Cashier and shopper in a small grocery. (78:1014:134)

89

90

91

89. Factory worker (making garlands?). (78:1014:66) **90.**
Stitching felt hats. (78:1003:26) **91.** Inspecting lens blanks.
(78:1014:51)

93

94

95

Garment workers. For Amalgamated Clothing Workers Union.
92. (72:159:419 mp) **93.** (78:989:41) **94.** (78:989:70) **95.** (78:989:
69)

96

97

Garment workers. For Amalgamated Clothing
Workers Union. 96. (72:159:422mp) 97. (78:989:25)
98. (72:159:426mp) OVERLEAF: 99. (78:989:32) 100.
(78:989:58) 101. (78:989:36) 102. (78:989:9; IMP NEG
12844) 103. (72:159:409mp)

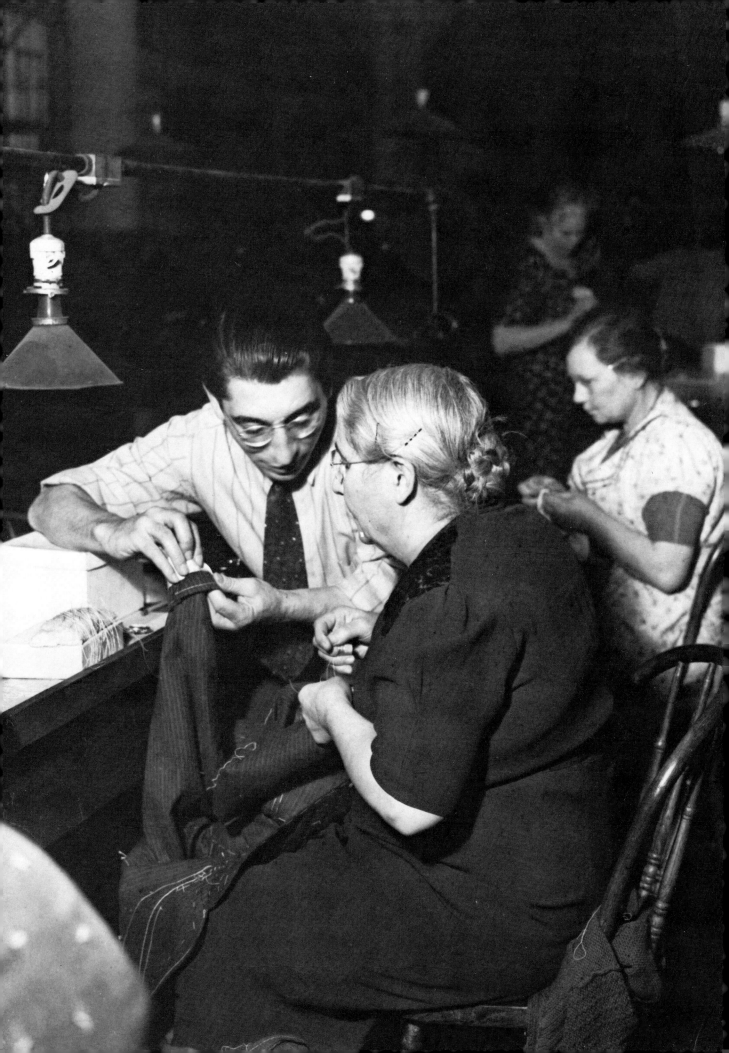

99

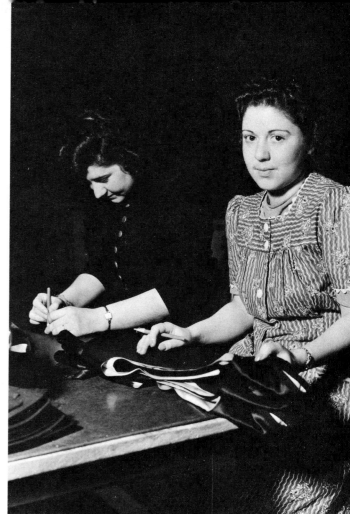

101 102

100

105

106

107

Garment workers. For Amalgamated Clothing Workers
Union. **104.** (72:159:403mp) **105.** (72:159:439mp) **106.**
(72:159:436mp) **107.** (72:159:415mp)

108

109

Garment workers. For Amalgamated Clothing Workers
Union. **108.** (72:159:414mp) **109.** (72:159:452mp) **110.** "72
yrs—40 at machine." (78:989:92)

111

112

113

For Shelton Looms. **111.** "Weaver in textile mill." (78:736: 16) **112.** Winder in a textile mill. (78:736:5mp) **113.** [Titles on various prints:] "A winder in a textile mill"; "A warper in a velvet mill"; "A bit of beauty behind the threads." (78:736: 122)

115

For Shelton Looms. **114.** "A young spooler, Shelton Looms."
(78:736:40) **115.** "Through the Threads. Hands of a textile
craftswomen in large silk mill." (78:736:18)

116

117

118

For Shelton Looms. **116.** Weaver in a silk mill. (78:736:35)
117. "A young 'winder' at the Shelton Looms." (78:736:3)
118. "Designing patterns for Shelton Looms — a large textile
Co." (78:736:14)

120

119. "Mrs. Sarah J. Wilson, Bulls Gap, Tennessee, 91 years old. In addition to daily work around the home, she finds time to raise some cotton, carding and spinning it herself. She also does some hand weaving. Oct. 22, 1933." (78:735:10)
120. "Pioneer grandmother in her farm home in the Appalachian Mountains." (78:735:3) OVERLEAF: 121. "Old plantation home in the South."(78:735:14)

122

122. "Boiling down sorghum at the Stooksberry homestead near Andersonville, Tennessee." (78:735:19) 123. "Aunt Lizzie Reagan, at the Pi Beta Phi School, Gatlinburg, Tennessee, weaving old-fashioned jean. Very few can weave this kind of cloth now. She is seventy-five years old and lives near the School, earning her living by weaving. Nov. 14, 1933." (78: 735:50) 124. "Old time spinner living up in the mountains of Tennessee." (78:735:60)

94

123

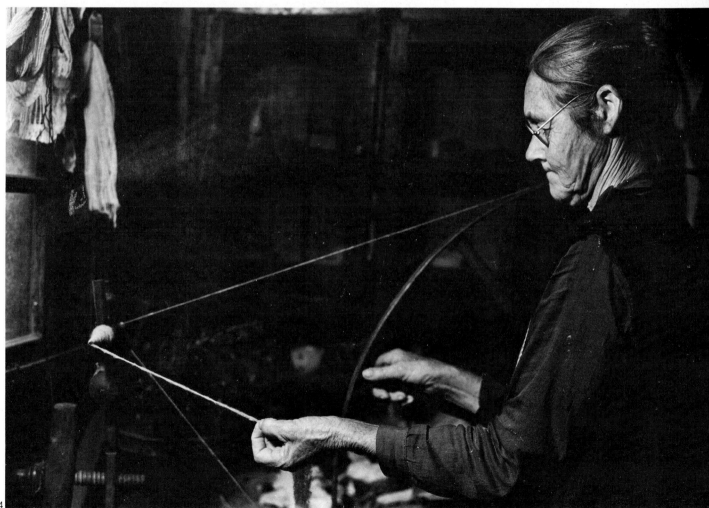

124

95

125

126

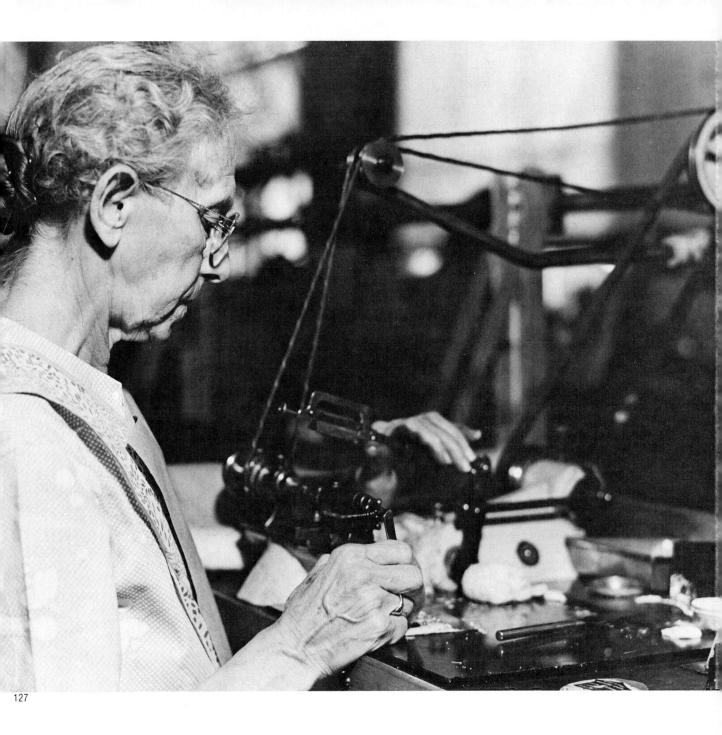

127

125. "Ruby Hilton, Lynn Gardens, Kingsport, Tennessee. Another view of the superfinish operation calling for the spraying of gold with an air gun. This girl has worked two to three years at the Kingsport Press. Nov. 10, 1933." (78:735: 47) 126. Examining clock parts (78:727:14) 127. "Life does not end at 40 for many workers. Wig Wag machine for polishing pivots. Watch factory, Pa." (78:727:25)

128

128. "Clocks." (78:727:3) 129. "Clock factory." (78:727:9)
130. "Worker in a clock factory." (78:727:16)

129

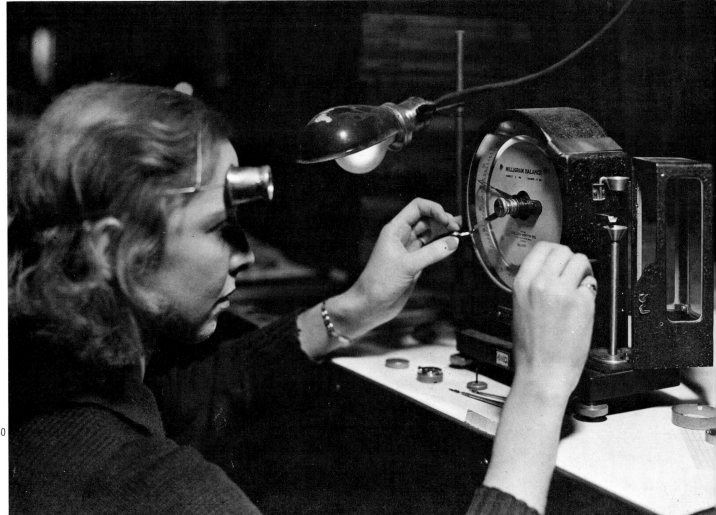

130

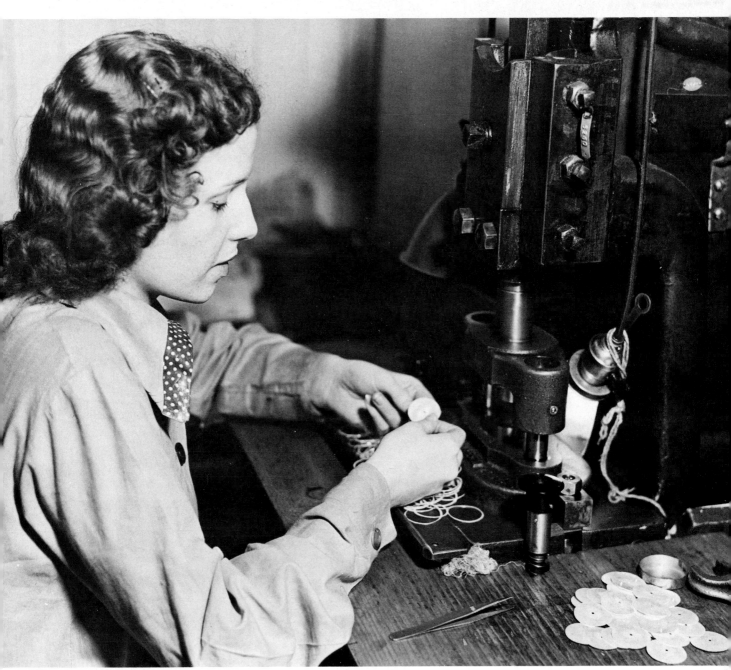

132

131. Workers in a clock factory. (78:727:44) **132.** Clocks."
(78:727:2)

133

134

133. Worker in a clock factory. (78:727:21)
134. "Watchmaker." (78:727:7)

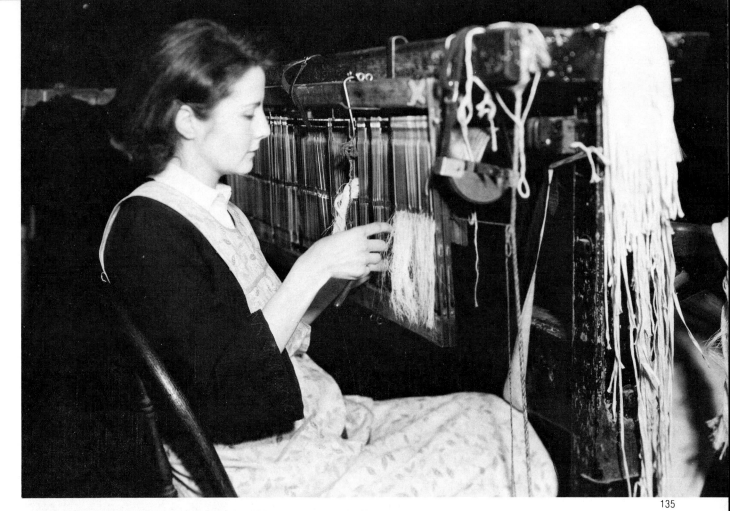

135

136

135. Textile Worker. (78:725:119) 136.
"A moment's rest for the spinner in a
North Carolina cotton mill. High Point,
N. Carolina." (78:725:77)

137

138

137. "Hand operated knot-tyer used on a winding machine. N.C. Textile Mill." (78:725:129) 138. Textile worker (78: 725:76) 139. "Speeder.—Frame hand doffing spools of speeder. High Point, N.C." (78:725:84)

140

140. Young girl working in a textile mill. (78:725:73)
141. Textile worker (78:725:117)

141

107

142

142. Textile worker. (78:725:63) 143. Textile worker. (78:725:66) 144. Textile worker. (78:725:61)

143

144

145

146

"Trio of ageing textile workers who keep up with the demands of increasing speed." **145.** "Polish worker at drawing frame." (78:725:59) **146.** "Doffing a roving machine." (78:725:75) **147.** "Piecing up on a fly-frame." (78:725:70)

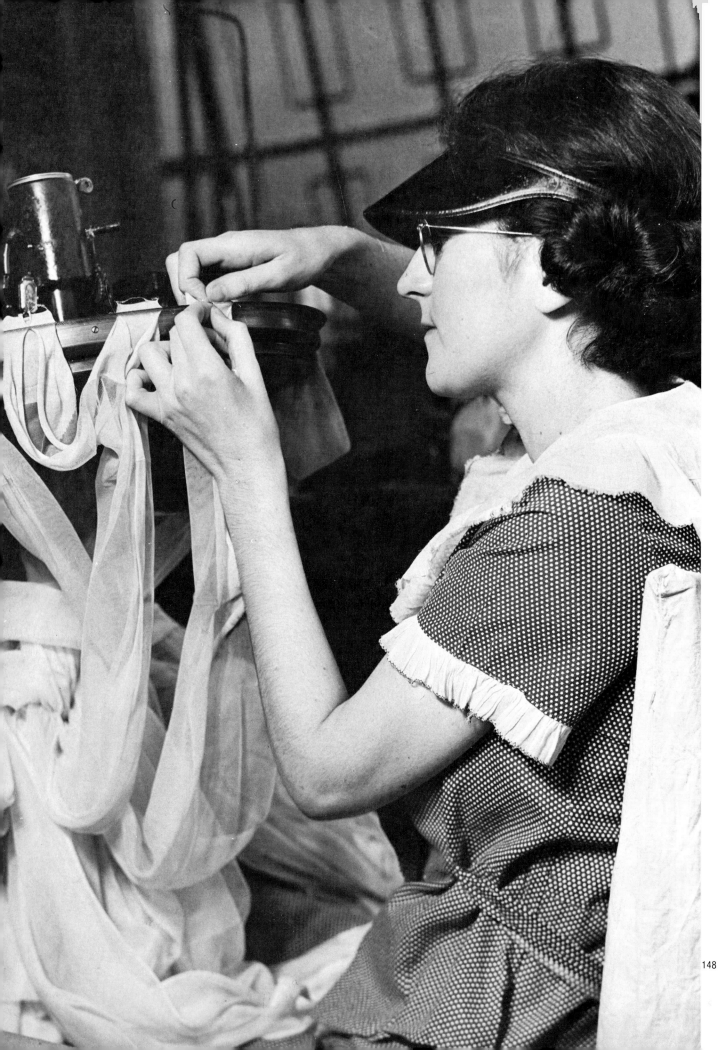

149

148. "Hosiery worker." (78:725:85) **149.** "Modern hosiery machine." (78:725:2)

150. Assembling radios. (78:732:1)

151. "A wash-and-tie girl tying stoppers to bottles. This is one of the few unskilled jobs for women in the glass factory. A wash-and-tie girl takes the bottle from the stopper grinders, washes it with automatic sprayers and ties the stopper to the bottle for packing." (78:726:36)

152. Polishing glass stoppers in a glass works. (78:726:49)